LITTLE BOOK OF

CITROËN 2CV

Ellie Charleston

CITROËN 2CV

First published in the UK in 2012

© G2 Entertainment Limited 2012

www.G2ent.co.uk

Printed and printed in China

ISBN 978-1-907803-43-7

The views in this book are those of the author but they are general views only and readers are urged to consult the relevant and qualified specialist for individual advice in particular situations. G2 Entertainment Limited hereby exclude all liability to the extent permitted by law of any errors or omissions in this book and for any loss, damage or expense (whether direct or indirect) suffered by a third party relying on any information contained in this book.

All our best endeavours have been made to secure copyright clearance for every photograph used but in the event of any copyright owner being overlooked please go to www.G2ent.co.uk where you will find all relevant contact information.

Contents

RIGHT Chic by name and chic by nature

Introduction

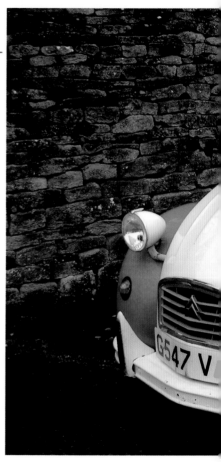

Tinsnail, pregnant skateboard, ugly duckling and umbrella on wheels are just some of the words that have been used to describe these quirky little French cars. And rather like Marmite™ you either love them or hate them. Personally I love them and have done so ever since I became aware of their existence holidaying in France over a quarter of a century ago. Then, just as now, I love how they stand out from the usual 'Euroboxes' that you see on the road today. Ok you may say they have no guts and throttle wide open they still struggle to reach the maximum speed limit on a motorway and it takes a day to go from 0-60mph. The 2CV or Deux Chevaux is a car that likes to gather speed rather than accelerate.

A convoy of 2CVs out on a run is something to behold especially if you catch them leaning precariously as they go round a bend in all their multi coloured glory. If you see them off road doing a '*Waggel*' where the driver turns

the steering wheel rapidly in succession left, right, left, right so that the car rocks violently, it might look as though the car is about to overturn, but these cars have fantastic road holding and will not roll over.

Summer-time when the driver of a modern car is wrapped in steel and cosseted by every gadget imaginable with the air conditioning blasting through, we will be pootling along with the roof rolled back enjoying the fresh air and hearing the birds singing. We will be enjoying the open road. But it is not just summer time when the car comes into its own. It's a perfect drive in snowy weather too. Front wheel drive and skinny tyres that cut through snow will ensure that we get to our destination, maybe not on time, but we will get there.

2CV owners are just as passionate about their cheap to run vehicles as are other classic car owners. The car may be a rust bucket and used every day or in concourse condition and kept in a heated garage and only brought out on high days and holidays but you can be sure that whatever condition it is in, it will be cherished.

No book could ever cover everything about this wonderful car but the Little Book of Citroën 2CV gives a potted history of the car and its derivatives, modcons, racing 2CVs and a taste of what it is like to be a 2CV owner.

A Brief History

The first 2CVs rolled off the production line in 1949 but the Citroën 2CV story begins much earlier with the legacy left by André Citroën. André Citroën was born in Paris in February 1878, the son of Lévie Citroën, a Jewish Dutch diamond merchant, and a Polish mother. Due to some failed diamond dealings, his father committed suicide when he was just a young boy and so had no influence on André's upbringing. André's time at school was uneventful and after graduating from the Lycée Louise le Grande in 1894, he studied engineering at the École Polytechnique but without any enthusiasm. He then spent a number of years in the French army as an engineering officer. Numerous stories abound as to how André Citroën first became aware of wooden helical gears but what is important is his interest in them. These gears used two sets of teeth in a 'V' or chevron shape and were used for driving water-driven machinery.

The fact that they ran quietly and were capable of high capacity power transmission without damaging the wood they were made from fascinated him. He realised that if such gears were made out of steel, their usage could be vastly improved and enlarged upon. He then set about designing just that and in 1904 filed a patent for steel double helical gears. He then set up a gear cutting business called La Société des Engrenages Citroën and used the chevron shape of the gears as his logo, the logo which we still associate Citroën with to this day.

By now, the car industry was well established in France and André Citroën's business met with success and flourished. At this point, he was asked to turn around the fortunes of Automobiles Mors which was struggling due to poor design and bad management. In 1908, André Citroën became chairman and set about changing working practices and brought in a system of mass production. Unfortunately for Automobile Mons, this was too little, too late and Citroën bought the factory in 1925 and Automobile Mons was no more. Citroën had been designing his own vehicles

FAR-LEFT
Helical gears
LEFT
André Citroën

bearing his name for about six years by now and with the purchase of the factory was able to carry on with this development. As he had done at Mors, so now he wanted to mass produce cars just like Henry Ford was doing in America, but war got in the way. When the First World War broke out, Citroën used his first factory, bought with the help of the Armaments Ministry, to manufacture armaments. This factory on thirty acres of waste ground on the Quai de Javel (later renamed Quai André Citroën) in Paris became his car plant after the war.

In 1919 the very first Citroën car was launched, this was uninspiringly called the Type A and as odd as it may now seem, was the very first French car to have its steering wheel on the left. It was a complete success and orders started to flood in. The break-even target for this car was 30,000 but within two weeks of its launch, orders for just over half that figure had already been reached and the target number of orders was reached before any car had even left the factory.

Further models followed including the Type B, the Model C and the

Cloverleaf. By now, André Citroën had undeniably built up a successful car manufacturing business; a business based on highly advanced engineering ideas and original concepts. He was also a master in publicity and used every means possible to advertise his cars. In fact, he had his own advertising department named, André Citroën Editeur. For nearly ten years from 1925 to 1934, the Eiffel Tower was transformed into a giant advertisement with the Citroën name shining into the night sky in illuminated letters up to thirty metres high that could be seen up to sixty miles away. A quarter of a million light bulbs were used along with 60km of electrical wiring. It is said that Charles Lindbergh, when at the end of his epic nonstop flight across the Atlantic used these lights to guide him to his destination at Le Bourget in Paris.

André Citroën bought advertising space in France's biggest selling papers and magazines and took out full page adverts and arranged for the Citroën logo to be splashed across road signs. In addition to this he had the foresight for the, what was then, innovative idea of setting up a network of dealerships, a spare parts catalogue, after sales service, a free service after running in and a one year warranty. Life was good and business was booming, but the depression was just around the corner.

During the 1930s and with harder times, in order to keep ahead of his competitors, André Citroën decided that what was needed was something new, fresh and exciting. In 1933, Citroën built the world's first mass produced front wheel drive monocoque car, the Traction Avant (the Maigret Car). Though this car stayed in production for twenty three years, its development caused Citroën's finances to become overstretched and practically bankrupted the company. The company's finances were not helped by André Citroën's very expensive gambling habit, losing personal as well as company money. André Citroën realising the enormity of the situation asked his friend Edouard Michelin if he would like to take over the company. The Michelin tyre company were already Citroën's largest creditors and with Michelin agreeing to this deal, the tyre company became the biggest shareholder of the Citroën business and André Citroën's was ousted.

LEFT
Citroën lights up the Eiffel Tower

André Citroën died in 1935 and never lived to see the car that this book is about.

Pierre-Jules Boulanger had worked for Michelin for some years and following the Citroën takeover, he was invited to become joint managing director and also chief of the design department. Boulanger was in fact an architectural draughtsman and not a car designer and had worked in a variety of jobs before joining Michelin. But in 1935, he set about turning the company around and initiated a design brief for the 'Toute Petite Voiture' (very small car) or TPV as it came to be known. The project itself became known as 'Béccassine'. This odd French name is rather derogatory as it a term for the wading bird, the snipe; yet it has also come to mean silly goose and is another way of saying fool.

The TPV was to be a simple, easy to maintain, affordable car, a car that would replace the horse and cart. In fact Boulanger asked his chief designer Maurice Broglie to design a 'motorised pony cart' for people who had no driving or mechanical experience. Originally Boulanger wanted the car

to have no more than three gears to make it simpler to drive but ultimately it ended up with a four speed gearbox that was quite an advanced feature on what was to become a very inexpensive car. Initially the fourth gear was marketed as overdrive and on early cars, the '4' was replaced by the letter 'S' to stand for 'surmultipliée' - en vitesse surmultipliée - in overdrive. The gear lever then and did right till the end of production come out of the dashboard horizontally. The gear shift pattern also stayed the same with first gear on the left, second and third gear in line and fourth gear or 'S' on the right as was also reverse. No !

Boulanger was a tall man so his design brief was for the creation of a car, well actually an umbrella on four wheels, that could travel at up to 35mph whilst carrying four people wearing hats, 50kg of produce – sheep, wine or potatoes - across a ploughed field with a basket of eggs on the front seat without breaking any of the eggs. He also requested that the car was frugal and would use no more than three litres of fuel per 100km and be able to travel at 60k per hour (35mph) fully laden. In addition, Boulanger was adamant that he

LEFT
Cyclops - the one eyed 2CV

1939   2 cv T.P.V

wanted the car to be as light as possible, yet as durable as possible and to cost far less than other cars available. This ultimately became the specification for the 2CV. The corporate headquarters of Michelin at Clermont-Ferrand then became the base for the TPV project.

Broglie entrusted the research and development to André Lefebvre, who had been the visionary behind the Traction Avant and the styling was given to Flaminio Bertoni. André Lefebvre was in fact an aeronautical engineer and worked for Gabriel Voisin, an aviation pioneer, designing military aircraft and later on building and racing competition cars before joining Citroën in 1933. He took over the Traction Avant project and became the technical brain behind the TPV project. Flaminio Bertoni began his working life as a carpenter in Italy and after his father's death he joined Carrozzeria Macchi, a carmaker as a coach builder. A disagreement at Carrozzeria Macchi forced a move to Paris with his wife. There, he had a succession of jobs including sculptor and designer but his skills attracted Citroën and in 1932 he joined the company where he was given responsibility for all

matters relating to design.

By 1936, Bertoni's design team had built a wooden prototype but Boulanger wasn't happy with it and various modifications were made. The following year, the first road going prototype had been built, a prototype that Boulanger approved of. The body of this prototype was made of aluminium on a tubular steel frame; the wheels were made of magnesium and the windows of mica. These materials were chosen in order to keep the weight of the car down. The interior was very basic with hammock-like seats suspended from the roof by cables; the roof itself was a piece of canvas stretching from the front windscreen to the rear bumper with

the small rear window incorporated in the canvas. Power came from a 500cc BMW motor cycle engine; this was simply because up to that point, the new purpose designed engine had not been tested. With the BMW engine, the kick-start was operated by the starting handle.

Over the next couple of years, very many variations to this prototype were built and in May 1939, Boulanger ordered 250 to be built at the factory in Levallois-Perret, Paris, a factory which had previously been occupied by Clément-Bayard, a bicycle, aircraft and automobile manufacturer. By August 1939, the final prototype was submitted to France's vehicle approval department with the target date for launch to be 1940. But the war put an end to that when Germany invaded France. The Citroën factory was placed under German control and Citroën had to suspend its plans for the TPV. Fearing that the Germans would discover their car, the French hid all of these prototype cars along with their plans and sketches. In 1940, Ferdinand Porsche who had heard rumours of the French car, one to rival his Volkswagen travelled to France to see it but Pierre

Boulanger refused to meet with him or to divulge any secrets to the enemy and so the prototypes remained hidden and unknown to the Germans.

Despite the German occupation, secret development of the car continued and further changes took place. The body was constructed out of the cheaper material of light gauge steel instead of aluminium, a single headlight was included – two were not legally required in France at that time, the doors did not have exterior handles and fully loaded the top speed was just 50 kilometres per hour. Very few prototypes were built as the basic raw materials were in short supply.

Once the war was over, the project, now named Cyclops due to the single headlamp, moved ahead in earnest but still the French kept their plans from the Germans. Further changes to the overall design took place and at times these moved away from Boulanger's original plans but he was a stickler and insisted that every detail was correct, sometimes, so the story goes, taking his family out for a test drive to ensure that the car details and expected fuel consumption were adhered to. It has also been said that he weighed the component parts of the prototype to ensure that they did not go over the weight of his original design brief. But the weight of the car did increase as essential items such as proper window glass and an electric starter were fitted. This did perturb him but he realised that it was necessary if the car was to become a commercial success.

Another aspect of the car that went through many permutations was the suspension. Remembering the original design brief for a car that could travel fully laden across a ploughed field, the design team decided to dismiss with what had been the earlier suspension system of torsion bars and go with an independent suspension system. The front wheels were connected to the back wheels by rods which were connected to a suspension spring. This gave a soft ride and allowed the car to lean at an alarming angle but without any fear of overturning. This basic principle stayed with the car throughout its life although conventional shock absorbers were brought in from the mid sixties onwards. The designers continued the tradition of front wheel drive that

had been pioneered with the Traction Avant. Citroën was the only company at this time manufacturing road going as against racing cars with front wheel drive and they chose this system due to its inherent safety and stability. They also used an air-cooled engine and unlike the rear engined VW Beetle, designed it so that it would be in the front of the car allowing for a good sized boot. Air cooled which has rather gone out of favour in modern times was chosen as the engine is much lighter and this was one of Boulanger's specifications. Air cooled engines do not require radiators and water pumps and this too saved on weight. Additionally in those early days, air-cooled engines tended to break down less and required less maintenance. The air-cooled engine was a winning formula and despite there being many changes in design of the car over the years, Citroën kept with this design. Another design feature that stayed with the car throughout its life were the very narrow wheels and tyres 125 x 15. This was another of Boulanger's idea so that the car with its generous ground clearance would be able to cut through mud, thus the ploughed field idea.

A BRIEF HISTORY

On 7th October 1948, at the Paris Motor Show a totally refined 2CV. for this was what the car now was, was ready to be shown to the world. The car, Model A, on display was nearly identical to the one that would be sold the following year. At Paris, the 2CV was the star of the show and attracted a great deal of controversy and interest both positive and negative. Much of the French press reported unfavourably about the car but, by all accounts, by the end of the show over a million people had visited the stand. The bonnet of the car though stayed firmly closed throughout the event as no decision had been made on what engine design should be favoured. Despite this, thousands of orders for this strange looking car were placed.

The French loved this value for money, minimalistic car. For the middle class Frenchman who had run small cars before the war, this was the perfect vehicle, cheap to buy, cheap to run, cheap to repair, spacious, comfortable and versatile with its fully roll back fabric roof which incorporated the boot lid. This canvas roof was advertised as a sun roof in later years but in the early

days it was seen as a means of getting large loads into the car. The back seat could be removed also to enable extra loads to be carried and it was designed in such a way that it doubled up as a picnic bench as well. The car featured suicide doors in that they opened backwards and a speedo cable that also drove the windscreen wipers. There were neither indicators nor a fuel gauge – the fuel was measured by a rod that was poked into the petrol tank via the filler cap. This dip stick was marked off in measurements and these indicated how much fuel there was left in the tank. Despite its lack of refinements, the French saw this car as one that could be used for pleasure and also as a work horse.

It was not until June 1949 that full production started. At the Paris Motor Show of that year, the ripple bonnet – a steel bonnet made of 23 narrowly spaced undulating grooves – was opened for all the world to see the horizontally opposed air cooled 375cc twin engine. With front wheel drive, independent suspension, rack-and-pinion steering and designed to give 9bhp at revs of around 3500 rpm, this was a car that captured the nation's heart.

Despite being popular, the initial production of the car was slow and the waiting period for delivery grew to up to six years. France was still struggling in the aftermath of the war and the raw materials and tools needed to build the car were in short supply. Production reached just 20,000 vehicles in the year following the start of full scale manufacture and though the French were passionate about the car, very few were able to realise their dream of owning one. Initially a permit was required to buy a 2CV and preference was given to vets, doctors, priests and farmers as it was reasoned that for the most part they had the greatest need and had to take priority. In fact in the early days, second hand 2CVs were in greater demand as they could be delivered sooner. People were prepared to pay a bit more to get one immediately rather than have to wait a number of years.

By 1951, the economic situation in post war France was improving and the Citroën factory was able to build 2CVs faster, but still not fast enough to keep up with demand and this situation continued right through to the mid fifties. Citroën gave the car a face

lift and added exterior door handles, door locks and an ignition key. At the Paris Motor Show of that year the Fourgonette was revealed, a van version of the 2CV, but more about vans later.

Due to the success of the car in France it was decided to produce a right hand drive version of the car for the British market. These cars were brought over from France as left hand drive versions and converted to right hand drive at the Citroën factory in Slough. Some of the cars were assembled in Slough and many of their constituent parts had to be sourced locally so that they would not be referred to as imports. These Slough built cars had a number of differences to their French counterparts. On the front doors, they had semaphore style flip up indicators that were self cancelling, which no previous 2CVs had had. In addition for the British market, the cars were given opening rear windows, special hub caps as well as a smooth metal boot lid instead of a totally canvas one. This boot lid was very much heavier than its French counterpart but it allowed a bigger window to be fitted which it was felt was what British buyers would

much prefer. Another item that Slough built cars had fitted was an ashtray, truly a luxury item and something that the French were interested in. French cars still had a single bench type seat at the front, but for the British market this was changed to individual seats. Furthermore the British public were given alternative choices of paint colour. All French built cars had been painted a metallic grey which at this time was changed to a semi gloss grey but the British were offered cars in grey as well as other colours including cream, green, blue, maroon and possibly brown. But all these anglicised refinements pushed up the purchase price of the car and in what started out as a cheap to run and cheap to buy car, ended up as a car higher in price than the average small British run-around. It was not just the price that caused the car to be a failure, parts of the Slough factory were shut down for a lengthy period and only limited numbers of 2CVs could be built.

One of the most distinctive and prized additions to Slough built cars was the badge, a 'Front Drive' emblem on the bonnet. Unfortunately this emblem doesn't fit modern bonnets due

to the shape. Many Slough built cars were exported, mainly to South Africa, Australia and New Zealand and a few survive to this day.

In total around 670 2CVs, 290 van conversions and some 70 pickups were built at Slough. Sales of Slough built cars completely ended in 1960 and right hand drive 2CVs did not appear again in Britain until 1974 when imports from France started.

In 1954, the basic 2CV engine was upgraded to 425cc and this enabled the car to reach the positively high speed of 50mph. In addition a centrifugal clutch was provided as well as flashing indicators, tartan material for the seats and a new catch system for the front windows so that they could be held open properly. By 1956, luxuries of a heater and demister were included and the rear window was enlarged.

Demand for the car remained high and its popularity had spread further than just Europe. Assembly plants were set up in places as far afield as Cambodia, the Ivory Coast, Chile and Argentina and as we see in a later chapter these and other countries produced their own versions of old favourites.

The 1960s saw a continuing evolution of the car in France including for the very first time a new paint colour. Up until very late 1959, buyers had been restricted to grey, but now they could buy a car in a pale blue or Glacier Blue as it was called. Over the decade, more and more new colours were introduced, generally still quite muted shades though. This was also the period when the ripple bonnet was discontinued and what is now seen as the modern bonnet with its five corrugations was introduced. The car no longer had suicide doors either; instead hinged doors with a handle on the inside were fitted. Other modifications included a third window on each side in the quarter panel; these are called '6 light' cars whereas earlier cars are referred to as '4' light. The 2CV had always been factory fitted with Michelin tyres but by the early 1960s, the tyre company had developed tubeless radials. They needed a car to demonstrate these new tyres on and the 2CV earned its place in history by becoming the very first car to be fitted with Michelin X radial tyres. This was the 60s, a period of great change globally and the times they were a changing.

The 2CV was struggling to keep up with a rapidly changing market and the 1970s saw some significant transformations to the car and one of the most noteworthy ones was the introduction of the 2CV4 with its 435cc engine and later the 2CV6 with its 602cc engine. The 602cc engine produced around 30bhp, a marked improvement on previous models. Seat belts were finally fitted to the front seats; this had been a problem for the British market as up till this point as it had been difficult to fit legal seat belts. Throughout the decade other changes took place including the upgrading of the electrical system from 6v to 12v, the fitting of hazard warning lights, changes in the headlamp shape as well as changes to the grille shape. Moreover, there were alterations to the hood fittings, air filter and also to the external trim. To keep the demand for new cars high, Citroën brought out a range of special editions, some of which will be covered in a later chapter. The 1970s also saw the introduction of the Dyane which was intended to replace what was

seen by Citroën as a dated car but as it turned out not by the buying public. The oil crisis in the 1970s spurred on more people to shy away from large gas guzzlers and move to the economical 2CV and once again the 2CV was in demand. An advert from around this time says it pithily "No wind-up windows. No retractable headlights. No cigar lighter. No turbo charge. No remote control door mirrors. No cruise control. No electric sunroof. No radiator. And then the punchline: "No wonder it's so reliable. There's nothing to go wrong."

Until now the cars had been fitted with drum brakes; these are known as 'drummers' but the following decade saw disc brakes being fitted as standard. In addition the number of different colours available was increased. Despite these changes, the French started to fall out of love with their little car. They were becoming a much more sophisticated nation and were moving away from being predominantly agrarian to urban. Their car requirements were changing and they wanted a conventional car with such features as a heated rear window, radio and cigarette

lighter and other modern accessories. They became more interested in the Citroën GSA, a typical city car of its time; the LNA a super-mini and later the CX and AX rather than the 2CV which by now was considered rather dated. New regulations were coming in with regard to safety standards and anti pollution laws and as the 2CV was a labour intensive and rather expensive car to manufacture, being hand built and hand painted, Citroën had some tough decisions to make. Demand for the car continued to fall and though it

back to the days of the peasant farmer and Citroën wanted to be seen as a high-tech car manufacturer.

The old and by now old fashioned factory at Levallois was closed down in February 1988 and production moved to the Mangualde plant in Portugal where labour costs were lower and the factory more modern. The very last car to roll off the Levallois factory was a grey 2CV6 Special. Almost as soon as production ended at Levallois, the factory was razed to the ground to make way for a housing estate.

But production only lasted for two years in Portugal and the cars that came out of Mangualde are considered inferior to French built models, mainly due to the poorer quality steel that was used. It is believed that between 40–45,000 cars were made at Mangualde. The 27th July 1990 was a sad day in the history of the 2CV when the very last car, a two tone grey Charleston rolled off the production line at Mangualde. In total over five million 2CVs were produced, not bad for a car that many considered ugly, fragile and unsuited to a modern lifestyle; one that has now become a proper classic cult car.

would have been possible to upgrade the 2CV to comply with these new rules, Citroën chose not to do so claiming that it wasn't financially able to continue building the car in France. In fact they were rather ashamed and embarrassed by the car as it harked

How The 2CV Got Its Name

The word 2CV stands for Deux Chevaux or two horses but the name 2CV really has little to do with horses. In France, the road tax system or Puissance Fiscale operated very much like the British

system prior to 1948 when a car was taxed on its horsepower. In France the CV or Chevaux Vapeur (steam powered horse) number is used to determine the road tax or vignette. Thus a car of less than 400cc would be in the 2CV class whereas a car such as the Traction Avant with its more powerful engines came in a number of CV classes including 15CV for its six cylinder version. There were very few cars in the 1CV class but the Renault Voiturette for example fell into this tax category. It had a 1 cylinder engine, which allowed it to reach a top speed of 20 mph. The original 2CV with its 375cc engine was designed to fall into the 2CV taxation bracket but the later 602cc engine cars were really 3CVs. Citroën took the decision to maintain the name 2CV throughout although the larger engined cars did become known

LEFT
The rare colour
scheme of navy
and cream

as 3CVs in Brazil. Ironically the road tax system was abolished in France and French-registered private vehicles no longer require a road tax certificate (vignette automobile), although it looks like the French government will be reintroducing car tax for very polluting cars in the near future.

Special Editions

The lower doors had a horizontal orange stripe on them with the word SPOT painted in the stripe. The interior of the car was finished in orange as were the seats and steering wheel, which incidentally was a different shape to the standard 2CV. An addition on this special edition was the inclusion of an orange and white striped sunblind fitted inside the hood. These cars were based on the 2CV4 and 250 were produced for the British market, one for each UK dealership. In total 1,800 of these distinctive cars were made. There are still a few originals in existence but they are a rarity on British roads.

The Spot

The Spot was the very first 2CV special edition. Introduced in the spring of 1976, Spot stands for **Sp**ecial **O**range **T**éneré. Its base colour was white but the hood and bonnet were painted in Orange Téneré. The Spot along with several other special editions was designed by Serge Gevin.

Le Basket

This special edition was the result of a competition given to a group of French students to develop a design that would represent youth and adventure. The design came out in 1976 and looked something like a blue, white and red basketball or tennis shoe with painted laces going across the bonnet

and painted vent holes along the side. This design inspired the Spanish 2CV Marcatello which was brought out in honour of the Spanish 1982 World Cup. Every single Marcatello had a 2CV82 logo on the boot. Officially only 300 examples were ever built, although the initial plan was for 500. Unlike the basketball car, this edition was painted red and white. But to the chagrin of owners,

the decals used on the body easily lost their colour in the Spanish sun and very few true Marcatellos now exist.

007

Another rarity is the 007. Designed by Serge Gevin and released in 1980, this is probably one of the rarest of the special editions, although technically it is not a special edition. The cars were originally

greatest James Bond chase scene of all time. The car that was designed for the promotion was painted in yellow with decals of '007' and also gun and bullet holes. People were interested in buying this unusual car, consequently the decals were supplied to Citroën dealers so that anyone purchasing a yellow 2CV had the option of buying these decals and converting their car to an '007' version.

In the film, various modifications had to be made to the car to improve its strength and speed. A complete frame within the car and under the floor had to be built so that the car could withstand being tipped on its side during the chase. In addition, the 602cc engine was replaced by one from a four cylinder GS which enabled Bond to escape his pursuers who were driving Peugeot 504s. In total three different 2CVs were used in the film. None were badly damaged and after filming they were sold on in a roadworthy condition.

Charleston

The next special edition to come out of the Citroën factory was the Charleston. These were out and out 2CV6s and they were produced as

to be used simply as an advertising ploy to be displayed in showrooms for exhibition purposes only. The car was produced following the release of the James Bond film 'For Your Eyes Only' where James Bond played by Roger Moore and his girl of the moment have to abandon Bond's Lotus Esprit in favour of a bright yellow 2CV in order to escape from the hit man Hector Gonzales. The film sequence featuring the 2CV topped a poll to find the a limited right hand drive version. Citroën initially wanted to produce just 8,000 examples but ultimately this art-nouveau styled car became a great success and a standard model.

The first batch of 400 was sold in 1981 and their colour scheme was black and red with a curved design painted on the sides. The initial batch was so successful that Citroën decided to produce a second version. This time they were brought out in three colour schemes – two-tone grey, black and red and black and yellow. The black and yellow version was a very limited edition coming out for less than a year and so it is quite unusual to see an original on the road.

Just like the Spot and '007' before, the very early Charlestons had painted rectangular headlamps, but these were soon changed to round chromed ones. There has been some confusion among the 2CV fraternity as to whether the rounded pattern on the car sides should be painted on or whether transfers should be fixed. It would seem that the early Charleston cars had their designs painted on the sides but from 1985, models were kitted out with decals. The

Charleston edition stayed in production for ten years and as we saw earlier, the last 2CV produced by Citroën was a two-tone grey Charleston.

Beachcomber

The Beachcomber or France 3 as it is known in France or 'Transat' in the

Netherlands was produced in 1983 in honour of the Citroën sponsorship of the French entry in the Americas Cup yacht race. In fact an agreement was reached whereby some of the profits from the sale of the car would help to finance the building of the yacht. The Beachcomber was marketed in Britain in a right hand version with 350 cars reaching these shores to begin with. The car was based on a standard 2CV6 but with a number of major differences. It was painted white with wavy blue lines along the sides, straight blue stripes on the bonnet, boot and roof. The wheels were also painted white and there was a special Beachcomber decal on the boot lid. In France, a picture of a yacht was added to this decal. Inside the car, the door panels were blue and the seats were upholstered in a specially designed white material with blue bands.

Dolly

The Dolly was the next special edition car to be made. The cars are actually called Dolly Spécials and they are all based on the 2CV6. The 2CV Spécials themselves had appeared in a variety of guises from 1976 onwards. The name 'Dolly' was chosen by the designer at Citroën who was working on these special editions. He was a great fan of a dance act involving twin sisters who worked at the Ziegfried Follies under the professional name of the 'Dolly Sisters'. This edition of the 2CV was

aimed at the female market and the Dolly name was considered a perfect lure. In early publicity it was marketed as a 'show business queen'!

The Dolly initially came out in 1985 in three different colour schemes. The first batch were red and grey, cream and grey and white and grey and these were followed by the second version of red and white, green and white and also cream and dark red which is affectionately known as 'plums and custard'. For the final series, navy and cream was added to the line up of red and white and green and white. The navy and cream cars, blueberries and cream, are a rarity as they were only produced for one year.

These cars were popular but it was very difficult for the dealers to quickly match the colour choice of car to the purchaser as these cars were built in batches of one colour only. Sometimes there was a shortage of one colour and a glut of another; so Citroën encouraged their dealers to change body panels to make unique cars. It has been known for a dealer to create a three coloured car with for example a cream bodyshell, red roof and green wings. These cars became known as Dolly Mixtures!

LEFT
The perfect wedding car

Club

The Club was in essence an ordinary 2CV but with rectangular headlights, seats that matched the body colour paintwork, a plastic grille and a differently shaped speedo. The Club came out in variety of colours.

Bamboo

The next special edition chronologically was the Bamboo. In 1988, this car with an all green bodywork, grey roof and white bamboo decals on both front doors and the boot appeared for the first time. It was in production for just one year and only ever appeared in Britain.

Cocorico

The Cocorico was the very last special edition launched in France. It was launched early in 1986 in honour of the World Cup that was going to be held later that year. Its advertising slogan was 'this 2CV is really too much'!

The Cocorico is one of the prettiest special editions with a blue merging through white to red colour scheme along the body with the words 2CV Cocorico written on the flap underneath the windscreen and also at the bottom of the boot; the colours representing the colours of the French flag. In the World Cup, France beat Brazil in the quarter finals and then went on to lose against Germany in the semis. Production of the Cocorico was limited to 1,000 cars but six months after its launch, there were still many unsold cars. Things might have turned out so differently if France had reached the finals.

Sahara

The 2CV had proved its potential as an excellent motorised pony cart and in the late 1950s; Citroën began to think about a true 4x4 car based on the 2CV to be in competition against the Jeep! The designers realised that the small engine that was fitted to the 2CV would not be adequate for serious off road use so they came up with the concept of putting a second engine in the boot. In 1958, they showed off their first prototype, a car with no hood and no holes in the doors. They later presented the car to the French Army and tried to convince them to buy them as they said that it would be a practical vehicle for the Army, but the Army did not take them

up on the offer. Further prototypes ensued with the body shape better resembling the Sahara that we know of today. Eventually one single design was more or less chosen and in late 1960, the Sahara proper was born. Two 425cc engines were fitted each capable of producing 12bhp which incidentally was upgraded to 13.5bhp on later models. Due to the two engines, the car needed two ignition switches and two chokes! Each engine could work independently of the other and in fact they were not linked but the engine in the front was considered the main engine. The boot lid had a hole cut into it to allow for air to be drawn in by the rear engine's fan. Other modifications to the standard 2CV of the time including the fitting of a spare wheel mounted in a recess on the bonnet, cut away rear wings and two fuel tanks beneath the front seats to cater for the car's higher fuel consumption. The car was advertised as being capable of climbing a sandy 40% slope fully laden and it would appear that this encouraged Swiss doctors in the Alps, oil exploration companies in deserts and allegedly the French Foreign Legion to buy examples. The name Sahara was

dropped in 1962 when Algeria gained independence from France and the car became known simply as the 4x4.

Just over 650 of these cars were built and though they were really considered a failure at the time, nowadays they are very much sought after by 2CV aficionados. They have been much copied but never bettered. Original models command exceptionally high sale prices with figures reaching €60,000.

Other Specials

In addition to the Citroën specials, a number of companies have used fleets of 2CVs for publicity purposes. One of the early ones was Perrier who in 1988 painted a series of 2CVs solely for the Belgian market. Just 1,000 of these 2CVs were ever built. They were based on a white 2CV with a Perrier green roof, a green squiggle and small green monkey on the bonnet. The monkey did pose problems for Perrier as it was considered a danger in the event of a collision with a pedestrian. Paradoxically the monkey's name was "Fhou" and came from a Perrier advertising campaign of the late 1980s 'Perrier c'est fou – Perrier that's crazy'.

LEFT
A Sahara

ABOVE
A Wella inspired
2CV

LEFT
Publicity for
Cochonou

In 1987, Wella, the hair products company used 2CVs for a promotion. The car they chose was a white one which they painted with their logo of dark brown waves down the sides of the car, to represent wavy hair. The cars were called Coco and they were used as prizes in their 'Coconut Balsam Treasure Trail'. It would seem that just two cars were ever made and were won in the UK. One definitely still exists but the search is still on to find out what happened to the second one.

In 1997, the kiwi fruit wasn't that well known in France and Zespri who were the importers to France of this New Zealand fruit wanted as many people as possible to get to know about it. The company decided that a road show lasting 70 days was the ideal way. A fleet of six 2CVs were painted in the green Zespri colours and they toured the country stopping off at 180 different places to publicise their fruit.

Cochonou, a supplier of French sausages and charcuterie were the official suppliers to the 1999 Tour de France. Instead of Fiat vehicles, they used 2CVs painted in the Cochonou corporate colours of red and white

check to follow the tour. To this day Cochonou still use the 2CV in their publicity as can be seen on their website: **www.cochonou.fr**.

To celebrate the 60th birthday of the 2CV in 2008, Hermès, the upmarket boutique, was commissioned to redesign the 2CV. Although they utilised a 1989 model, they chose to use the classic front bench seat rather than individual seats. In addition they repainted the entire car in an exclusive brown, added leather trim to the door, to the gear knob and sun visor as well as to the steering wheel. The roof of the car which is normally a vinyl type material featured a Hermès cotton canvas that matched the interior trim.

As well as standard colours or specially designed publicity cars, at any 2CV gathering you will also see cars painted in a multitude of colours often to reflect the owner's personality. If you are lucky you may also see some cars completely covered in unusual materials. I have seen cars covered in plastic bags from a major supermarket, beer bottle tops, beer labels and even carpet. Nothing is beyond the imagination of a 2CV owner.

2CV Vans

From the early 1950s through to the late 1970s, Citroën brought out a series of 2CV vans in tandem with the cars. These vans were extremely popular commercially and were used for carrying all sorts of objects as well as being used by the ambulance, fire and postal services. The front half of the van was just like the car but the rear half was totally different. Initially the vans were built with narrow corrugated sides, manufactured

by Panhard but as changes in design were made over the years, one change that was inevitable was the removal altogether of the side ripples in order to facilitate sign writing.

The very first French van was shown at the 1950 Paris Salon (Motor Show) and it was available for purchase from 1951. The van was known as the Fourgonette and it came with the 375cc engine, the same that was in the saloon version of the 2CV. One difference to the saloon was that the van was fitted with a centrifugal clutch rather than the Trafficlutch. It was not until the early 60s that the Trafficlutch was fitted as an

ABOVE
In the snow outside the Tan Hill Inn, the highest pub in England

LEFT
Citroën corporate colours decorate this 2CV van

longer in the cargo bay than the AZU and it was fitted with the 602cc engine and chassis from the Ami 6, although this did change in 1968 when the M28/1 engine was fitted. The AK also featured larger side windows behind the front seats. The AK400 built from 1970 onwards was even higher and heavier than the AK350 weighing in at some 50kg more and being some 16cm higher. These were never sold in Britain although a few right hand drive versions were made for the Belgian postal service.

The 2CV Mixte is one vehicle that is neither saloon nor van. In fact, as its name implies, it is halfway between the two. The early 60s saw the first appearance of the Mixte with a boot lid that included the back windscreen and a part of the roof and consequently opened like a hatchback. Other peculiarities of the Mixte included a removable rear seat and also the fitting of the spare wheel under the bonnet. The Mixte was replaced by the Commerciale which had a flatter boot floor.

In total over a million 2CV vans were built before they were replaced by the Acadiane van.

option. These vans came with small oval shaped windows in the rear doors, but no windows in the side panels plus a wing mirror.

In 1955, the AZU (250) van was brought out, with the U standing for Utilitaire or Utile. The engine was increased to 425cc and the narrow side ripples of the cargo bay were changed to wider corrugations. The very last AZU 250 was made in 1978. The next van was the AK350 built for seven years from 1970. The AK was some 20cm

Royal Marines Pick-ups

In the 1950s, the Royal Marines were testing a number of different helicopters to discover their potential as a search and rescue, assault as well as lift vehicle. It must be remembered that this was still in the early days of helicopter design and just ten years after Sikorsky started full production of its helicopter. The Royal Navy wanted to do some test transport lifting and they looked at the various vehicular options available. Land Rovers and trucks already used by the Royal Navy were considered too heavy as the limit of the helicopter cargo hook was set at around 540kg. A vehicle that just a few men could lift should the need arise was required. What was crucial was for it to be light, robust and easily modified. A 2CV van from a garage near Chichester was chosen. The vehicle was an ordinary van without any

modifications. Various test flights were made over the Solent with the 2CV slung under the helicopter and the 2CV proved to be tough and was returned to the dealership undamaged. An order was then placed at the Slough works for a 2CV pick-up. The 2CV pick up with the registration number 33CPP was put through its paces in various manners and as it was considered the ideal vehicle, an order for four further pick-ups was made. These ones had slight modifications for the military and were painted a greeny bronze colour.

33CPP was used onboard the aircraft carrier HMS Bulwark and travelled around the world a bit, never actually doing any serious service. There were occasional sea tests but that was about it. Meanwhile the other four pick-ups were sent to such diverse places as Malta, the Middle East and Italy.

ROYAL MARINES PICK-UPS

They were lifted by various helicopters and occasionally damaged and one was deliberately ditched into the sea. Despite this, thirty five more pick-ups were ordered from Slough to serve as transport for the Royal Marines once they were on land. Most of this allocation was put into service aboard HMS Bulwark. Unfortunately the helicopters that were used to lift the vehicles off the decks often struggled to get off the ground themselves and with a 2CV slung underneath them, this occasionally became nigh on an impossibility. The 2CVs were stripped of all but their essential equipment to ensure that they were as light as possible. This did have the added advantage that without windows and doors, once on land, the troops could fire on the enemy more easily.

Helicopter construction had improved when HMS Albion, the sister ship to HMS Bulwark went to the Far East in 1961. She carried a cargo of another thirty 2CV pick-ups, again to be used as transport for the Royal Marine commandoes. Once again a number of cars were written off during exercises but most of HMS Bulwark's cars were put ashore in Singapore and Malaysia soon after they were demobilised. In total it is believed that 131 special pick-ups were built for the Royal Marines and that just three still survive.

Close And
Distant Relations

Ami 6 And Ami 8

In the late 50s, Citroën was in a quandary, it had updated the styling of the 2CV but nothing could change the fact that it was essentially a very basic

car. It was also selling the sophisticated DS but these two cars were poles apart. Citroën decided that what its dealerships needed was something that would plug this gap, a super 2CV and so the Ami 6

BELOW
An Ami with matching trailer

was born. It was introduced at the Paris Salon in April 1961 and though it was less rounded than the 2CV, opinions were divided on its sleeker shape. It had inward slanting rear windows, somewhat like the Ford Anglia but there the similarities ended. The British didn't take to the car and in fact it was rarely seen outside France. Over a million cars were built but less than a thousand ever made it to Britain. There are a few right hand drive models that were special imports. Citroën even forced an estate version on the British public in 1966 but though this appealed to the French family, it again proved unattractive to British drivers.

Advertised as 'the world's most comfortable medium-sized car', it's surprising to discover that it shared many components with the 2CV, components such as the engine, suspension, gearbox and chassis. The Ami 6 was the first car to be built at Citroën's new plant at Rennes-le-Janais in Brittany and by 1965 more Ami 6s were being built than 2CVs. The Ami 6 came out in a number of variants including the Tourisme or Comfort and Club. Despite its popularity in France, by 1969 production of the Ami 6 ceased entirely and in its place came the Ami 8. One idiosyncrasy about the Ami 6 is that it is the only Citroën car where the Citroën logo of the double chevron was never visible from the outside.

Launched at the Geneva Motor Show, the Ami 8 was exactly the same as the 6 engine wise but it was given a new body and with that modifications were made to the cabin. In 1969 though, the Ami 8 was supplied with inboard disc brakes, the first A series vehicle to have them fitted. In the autumn of 1972, the Ami Super was introduced in Berline (saloon), Break (estate form) and Enterprise (van) forms. These cars with a 1015 cc air cooled engine taken from the GS range and a top speed of around 87mph were put in the 6CV fiscal bracket.

One very rare version of the Ami 8 is the M35 which was launched in 1969. The M35 had a totally different body to either the 6 or the 8; it was a 2 door coupé, built as an experiment to discover its feasibility. The M35 had a 995cc longitudinally mounted Wankel rotary engine which gave a maximum speed of 90mph. The engine itself was supplied by Comotor SA which was a company formed by a collaboration between Citroën and NSU. The body was built by Heuliez and though it was on an Ami 8 base, there were very few common parts between the two models. A unique feature of the car was that this was the only 'A' series vehicle ever to be equipped with hydraulic suspension.

The M35 was supplied to loyal and valued Citroën customers for them to comment on how practical it was in high mileage situations. All repair and maintenance tasks were performed by a team of specialists from Citroën's research and development department who kept records on each engine's performance.

The plan was to build 500 of these cars but ultimately only 267 were ever built and each one was individually numbered on the front wings. Sadly, all this took place just as the 1970s oil crisis was beginning to have an effect and as these Wankel engines were very thirsty, Citroën decided to abandon the project. At the end of the experiment, most of the cars were recalled by Citroën and subsequently scrapped. In spring of 2011, a garage in the Netherlands claimed to have discovered fourteen of these cars in a Dutch warehouse. Included among these which had been secreted away was one of the super rare 122. This was one of only three M35s made in blue, allegedly the favourite colour of Heuliez himself.

Dyane And Acadiane

In the mid sixties, despite the 2CV being a success, Citroën decided that what was needed was a successor and possibly a total replacement to the 2CV. The Dyane or AY which was its codename during the research years was aimed as an intermediate model between the 2CV and the Ami and in direct competition with the popular Renault 4. Right from the outset the decision was made to build a hatchback style car and although the Dyane is built on the chassis of the 2CV and has many identical components, it is an entirely different car.

The Dyane first shown at the 1967 Paris Salon was much more angular than the rounded 2CV and its bodywork was wider. In addition it had much larger windows, recessed headlights, a fully opening tail-gate yet it retained the 2CV 425cc engine. When the car was actually launched in 1968, it was available in two forms, the Confort and the Luxe. The very first cars were fitted with the flat twin 4 stroke 435cc engine, but soon after the launch a 602cc engine car was

brought out. These cars became known correspondingly as the Dyane 4 and Dyane 6. In 1970, the 602cc engine was uprated and this enabled the car to reach speeds of almost 70mph and it could go from 0-60mph in about half a minute!

The very first Dyanes came out without any windows in the 'C' pillar but by 1970 small side windows were fitted into these rear panels. Initially all Dyanes were fitted with drum brakes but these were replaced by disc brakes in 1977. A couple of years later, the small metal fuel tank was replaced by a plastic fuel tank with a capacity of 25 litres. Various other minor modifications were made throughout the Dyane's life such as in 1973 when the door handles were mounted the other way round or the fitting of a new plastic grille with

horizontal bars in 1975.

A number of different Dyane versions were built and one of the prettiest is the Caban or as it is sometimes known Cabane. In 1977,

1,500 examples of the Dyane Caban were manufactured. The Caban was mainly for the French market although it did appear in other countries notably Britain, Switzerland and Germany. It is a very stylish car with a dark blue body, white wheels with chrome hubcaps, a white roof and delicate white stripes on the doors, bonnet and hood and special plaid upholstery. Each car is numbered on the lower left of the bodywork. According to Citroën advertising, 250 cars were reserved for the Swiss market with the first 20, which were numbered 1 to 20, to be won in a raffle.

Other limited editions of the Dyane include the Capra, Edelweiss, Côte d'Azur, Argent and Nazaré as well as the Dyane van, the Acadiane.

Both the Capra and the Edelweiss were built for the Spanish market and as far as can be ascertained only 600 examples of the Capra and 750 of the Edelweiss were ever built. Both these cars were launched in 1981. The Capra came in just one colour, yellow and like the Caban each model was numbered. The Edelweiss came in blue. No one seems to know why these colours were chosen as the Edelweiss is a delicate white flower. The Nazaré and Argent were built for the Portuguese market as Nazaré is a fishing village in Portugal, but why that particular town was chosen is subject to conjecture. Little is known

about these two cars although we do know that they came in at least three colours, yellow, beige and blue. The Côte d'Azur was built in the early 1980s and many were exported to the UK. The Côte d'Azur came in white with turquoise blue coach lines.

In Iran, a version of the Dyane called the Jiane, Jian or lion was built. They were built in a joint venture between Citroën and Iran National until the 1979 revolution and after that they were built without any involvement from Citroën.

In addition to the special edition models, Citroën also introduced the much loved Acadiane in 1978. This was a hybrid vehicle with the front end of a Dyane and a lengthened and strengthened rear end of the 2CV van which at that time was the AK. Even the name was a mixture of the two vehicles AK and Dyane. The Acadiane was built at the Citroën factory in Vigo Spain for just ten years but in that time over a quarter of a million vehicles were produced.

The Dyane went out of production in 1983, several years before the demise of the 2CV, the car it was meant to replace.

Méhari

Citroën had already taken a foray into the world of 4x4s with the Sahara but their next project for a vehicle capable of off-roading was the Méhari, a jeep like car. The Méhari was named after the breed of dromedaries used by the Berber tribesmen of North Africa for long distance travel.

The very first Méhari was launched in 1968 and although it was based on the Dyane 6, its body was made of acrylonitrile butadiene styrene, or ABS. This is a common material nowadays but then it was quite innovative and it was the first time that ABS had been used in a production car. There were thirteen individual body panels that made up the vehicle and these were made by the SEAB group of Villejuif who attached them to the Citroën chassis. The cars were not painted; instead pigment was added to the ABS during manufacture. This was fine in cool countries but if the cars were subjected to hot sun, the ABS had a tendency to become brittle and crack and develop small stress lines, so they were protected with UV paint. On the plus side, as the ABS was self coloured, small scratches and knocks were difficult to see. The Méhari was very basic and lacked doors and seat belts; the only protection was a simple canvas roof with side screens although by 1971 a hard top did become available.

Only one special edition of the Méhari was ever made and it was called the Azur. The Azur was marketed as a beach buggy and came in the maritime colours of white with blue and white striped seats.

In late 1979, early 1980, the 4x4 version of the Méhari was released. These cars had disc brakes on all four wheels and the spare wheel was fitted in the bonnet. Four wheel drive was delivered through a reduction gearbox and a differential lock on the rear axle. This gave the car seven forward speeds and great capability in difficult terrains. Unfortunately the 4x4 Méhari only lasted just over three years and the final one rolled off the production line in 1983. The Méhari ceased production in 1987 after 140,000 plus vehicle had been made.

A number of other Jeep like 2CV based vehicles have been built including the Yagán from Chile. This vehicle was

LEFT
Full weather gear on a Méhari

CLOSE AND DISTANT RELATIONS

named not as some believe after an Aborigine warrior tribe, but after a group of indigenous people from Chile. It would appear that the Yagán was commissioned by the then President Salvador Allende to be used by troops to patrol the streets after the Chilean coup of 1973. Each Yagán was a truly unique vehicle as they were built entirely by hand without any patterns and so no two vehicles are identical. Although they were based on the Méhari, they were made of metal and were much squarer and many would say far uglier.

A similar car sold in several West African countries was the Baby Brousse. This was another car which was originally based on the Ami 6 chassis but it was made out of a pressed steel body that required no welding and was bolted to the chassis. The development of the Baby Brousse is quite odd as Citroën actually bought the licence to build the cars from two Frenchmen in the Ivory Coast. Citroën's plan was to put the car into production in other countries and in fact the Dalat, a similar vehicle was built in South Vietnam. The Dalat had a square grille and Dyane headlights. Both these cars had innumerable

CLOSE AND DISTANT RELATIONS

changes made to them during their life span owing to difficulties in obtaining components.

In Greece, a jeep like car was built by Namco (National Motor Company of Greece). Named the Pony, this vehicle was a collaboration between Namco and Citroën using the 2CV/Dyane as the base model. The car was constructed in a factory especially built for the purpose and it was first introduced at the Thessaloniki Trade Fair in 1972. Due to its robust construction and versatility, this car was a big hit. Its success was also helped by favourable tax legislation for small cars. The car was produced for nine years and over that time several improvements and changes were made to keep it up to date. Several other Greek manufacturers tried to emulate the success of the Pony by building their own versions but no other car came anywhere near its popularity.

Another version of a jeep like Citroën was the FAF (*Facile à Fabriquer* et *Facile à Financer* - easy to manufacture and easy to finance). The car was aimed at third world countries as it was easy to manufacture. Made of

steel, the intention was that imported materials would not need to be used. In fact the aim was for at least 50% of the components to be sourced locally thus reducing import duties and the need for major investment and also to provide work for local people. According to Citroën's own factory documentation of 1978, they intended the car to come out in two version, 2 wheel and also 4 wheel drive, with the latter designed as an all terrain vehicle that could be used in sandy, muddy or slippery conditions.

Not dissimilar to the FAF was the ill-fated Africar, a British design concept using the 2CV gearbox and also the Bedouin, another British manufactured car. Neither of these cars set the world alight. In fact only one Africar seems to have ever been fully made and the Bedouin was a short-lived project.

The Vanclee of Belgium is another Méhari styled car, usually seen with a hard top. Production began around 1978 and ended some ten years later. The Vanclee came out in two designs, the Mungo and the Emmet and the very first Emmet that was sold was in pick-up form.

Bijou

'The smartest, most comfortable, most economical small car of the year' was how Citroën described the Bijou, a car aimed at the British people and built in England. This car was introduced to a stunned British public at the 1959 Motor Show in London. At that time the British hadn't yet fallen in love with the 2CV and Citroën decided that what the British needed was an adapted 2CV.

The Bijou was the only car built and designed outside France being built at the Citroën factory in Slough between 1959 and 1964. Unlike the metal bodied 2CV, the Bijou was made of polyester resin reinforced glass fibre styled by Peter Kirwan-Taylor who worked with Colin Chapman of Lotus and found fame as the designer of the Lotus Elite. The Bijou was a two seater, two door saloon with a very small backseat which

could be folded down. Its big selling point was that it had an extra large lockable boot! The engine that went in the Bijou was the two cylinder 425cc engine from the 2CV. Most though not all Bijoux were fitted with a centrifugal clutch. The Bijou was fitted out with other luxuries including an ashtray, front parcel shelf and low fuel warning light. Despite an impressive 60mph, the British did not fall in love with this peculiar car at all and only around 207 were ever built with possibly a couple of prototypes as well.

H Van

The H van is not really an 'A' series derivative but it has a close bond with the 2CV, well it does share the same headlights! So much could be written about these large vans that that would fill an entire book in itself.

The H van proper was launched in 1947 at the Salon de l'Automobile in Paris. When full commercial production began the following year, the vehicle was referred to as the Type H. This was a four cylinder, front wheel drive vehicle with a 1911cc water-cooled engine and a six volt electrical system with a payload of 1200kg. The following year a slightly smaller version, the HZ, came out with a reduced payload of 850kg. In the 1950s this was further increased on the HY to 1500kg and then over the years various models with greater and lesser payloads, longer and shorter wheelbases, extra height, and different engines including a Perkins diesel came out from time to time.

The very first H vans were built at the Javal Citroën factory but later models were also built in the Netherlands, Belgium and Portugal. Despite many subtle changes in design

throughout its life, the H van always maintained its corrugated panelled body. It came out in three versions, van (fourgon), cattle truck (betaillere) and pick up (plateau) and so it was used for all sorts of purposes – ambulances, fire engines, police vehicles, delivery vehicles, mobile shops, catering vehicles and even mobile laboratories. To this day you can still see conversions to hot food vehicles, cafés, mobile work shops and of course one of the most favoured conversions, campervan.

By 1981 the very last H van rolled off the production line at Aulnay. In total nearly half a million H vans had been built during its 34 year life. Citroën UK did toy with the idea of producing a right-hand drive version but it would appear that only three such vehicles were ever built. The H Van was succeeded by the H15/25 in the mid seventies, a much more run of the mill design.

Modcons

2CV owners like to drive individual and unique cars and the market in kit cars based on the 2CV platform has waxed and waned over the years. Drivers often choose to drive a kit car because they are exciting and distinctive and look different from the majority of other cars on the road. Plus of course there is a certain amount of satisfaction and sense of achievement to be gained in driving your very own car after hours and hours of hopefully not too much frustration in building it.

Black Jack Avion

The Black Jack Avion was created by Richard Oakes in 1995. Oakes also designed the Midas, Pegasus and GTM Libra. The Black Jack Avion is a light, racy sports car made of a polyester body moulding and as its name suggests looks a bit like a plane obviously without the wings. The base car has three wheels and uses the 602cc engine, clutch, and transmission along with the rack and pinion steering and suspension from the 2CV, but not the chassis. There is a comprehensive list of options that can be added including special 16" polished stainless steel wire wheels with aluminium hubs, a glass fibre petrol tank, a tonneau cover, anti roll bar and even an aluminium dashboard; accordingly every car can be unique and the owner can embed their own personality into the vehicle. Despite being air-cooled just like the 2CV, the Black Jack is not fitted with a cooling fan; instead the cylinders are on the outside which is enough to keep them cool. It is estimated that it takes about 200 hours to build a Black Jack although at one point they were available from Black Jack as a whole vehicle. It is believed that around fifteen vehicles a year were sold with total sales somewhere in the region of between sixty and seventy.

Burton

Imagine a 2CV with gull wing doors - well that is precisely what the Dutch brothers Dimitri and Iwan Göbel did.

ABOVE
A brand new
open 2-seater
Burton

These two brothers established their company first in 1993 calling it 'Duck Hunt Car Design' and then in 2000 they renamed it the Burton Car Company. In 1998 they began to design what eventually became the Burton but which they code-named 'Hunter'. The idea behind the Burton is very simple;

remove the body from a 2CV but keep the chassis, engine and much of the running gear and fit a new polyester body. Any 2CV or Dyane can be used as a donor vehicle, preferably one that is a rust bucket though.

The Burton is a two seater car and it comes in a choice of hardtop with gull wing doors or a custom made convertible roof. Full windscreens or aero screens are available. Luggage space is vast in the Burton considering the size of the donor vehicle with a large rear boot and also a smaller storage area under the bonnet. The body colour is impregnated into the material and there is no limit to what colours can be chosen. Wheels can be standard 2CV wheels or special Burton ones. The choice of styling knows no bounds. In addition, the car is available in a variety of build forms, provide the donor car yourself, buy the rolling chassis or get Burton to build the car of your dreams.

The Burton is surprisingly fast bearing in mind that the engine is the basic 602cc; this is because the car is light and has a good aerodynamic shape, but of course fitting bigger cylinders, a racing camshaft and a lightened flywheel will all improve the performance.

Charon

The Charon, named after the ferryman in Greek mythology is a car rarely seen on Britain's streets. It is made in Holland and is another with sports car styling, although the Charon definitely looks like a car from the 1930s. The first cars,

all based on the 2CV were built in the mid 1980s without doors, but since then the options of doors and a hood have been added. Just like the Burton, the Charon is available in kit form and also as a complete car.

Cogolin

This was a one off conversion made by Colonel Hourcastagne of the French fire service in the 1950s. The story goes that one night while on duty, he was trying to attend to a fire and driving along a mountain road at some point in the journey, the road became blocked and the Colonel couldn't turn round on the narrow road. He was forced to reverse back down it with just another fireman and a torch to guide him. As a result, Colonel Hourcastagne decided that what the fire service needed was a car that could drive in both directions! As crazy as this may seem, the fire service did buy two 2CVs and welded the front sections together to form one car. Each section was able to function independently as each had its own 425cc engine although the engines were not connected. In fact one engine can

pull the car in first gear while the other pushes in reverse.

In 1952, the French coachbuilders Ansart & Teissere built the Cogolin and it stayed in service with the fire department for twenty years. At present, the car is on display at the Lane Museum in Nashville, Tennessee. Though this was a unique vehicle, since then several people have built their own version of the Bicephale (two heads) and replicas can be seen from time to time at shows or events.

Dagonet

During the 1950s, Jean Dagonet, the French racing driver and also coach builder was interested in improving the performance of the standard 2CV. He decided to test a new type of carburettor and fitted it to six cars which were then driven around France in what became known as the first Tour. In addition to this, he built a number of conversions of the 2CV in his factory in Rheims. One of the most striking conversions was the one he completed in 1956 where the very sloping roof was solid rather than canvas and the entire back window was incorporated into the hood. The body was dramatically lowered in height and widened to alter the centre of gravity and also had its weight reduced by the addition of a GRP body. Additionally the Dagonet was fitted with two carburettors and two exhausts. These conversions are extremely rare and it is very unusual to see the genuine article.

Deauville

Unlike the previous cars, the Deauville Canard does not have a sports car look. In fact if anything it is an attempt at presenting a car that resembles the pre-war years with a very long bonnet, running boards and a pram like hood. The Deauville was conceived in Britain although it was exported to many European countries. Both the Deauville Mark 1 and Mark 2 were intended to use most of the parts from the original donor 2CV apart from the body. The Deauville body is made of GRP (glass reinforced plastic) and is finished in a grey primer ready for painting. Frequently it is painted in a two tone combination that perfectly suits its retro styling. In addition to the Canard, Deauville recently brought out the Martlet and the Canjtio. The Martlet is a bolt on section that fits to the rear of a standard 2CV, minus its rear boot section, and converts it into a van, again with retro styling. In complete contrast the Canjito is a Méhari style car that comes with four full seats, hood and side windows.

Falcon

The Falcon came in either three or four wheel formation and was inspired by Colin Chapman of Lotus. In fact, despite using the floor pan and engine of the 2CV, the car really does have a Lotus 7

look about it. The main body of the car was built of plywood with the bonnet, wings and boot being made of GRP. To individualise their cars, some owners fitted stainless steel or aluminium panels over the plywood. The basic car came in red, British Racing Green, Oxford Blue, yellow, black or white or any combination of these colours. Around 200 of these cars were built.

Hoffman

This kit car is unlike the others insofar as it is a cabriolet and a very nice-looking one at that, although there is nowadays the option of a hard top.

Wolfgang and Felix Hoffmann of Bavaria, Germany developed the kit for a 2CV conversion in the late 1980s. The car retains many of the features of its donor 2CV but the body is made of GRP and consists of just two side windows. Many Hoffmanns have been built and it is believed that in total around 2,000 conversion kits have been supplied.

Le Patron

Le Patron is another sports car style conversion with a very long bonnet, not dissimilar to the Lomax, which is the next car mentioned in this section.

Le Patron has been developed in the Netherlands since 1998 although the company involved has been creating kit cars since 1991. Le Patron uses the chassis, running gear and engine of the 2CV. It is rare to see this car in Britain as most have been built on the continent, predominantly the Netherlands, Germany, Belgium, France and Spain. The name of the car comes from André Citroën's nickname – he was often referred to as 'Le Patron' (the chief).

Lomax

Lomax stands for: 'Low Costs, Maximum Performance' and the Lomax is probably the most frequently seen 2CV kit car conversion in Britain. It comes in a variety of forms, both three-wheeler and four- wheeler. The three wheel version or 223 is a very popular model that was inspired by Morgan. Obviously only a 2-seater it has some storage space although not a great deal; most of this is behind the seats although many owners do fit a luggage rack to the boot. The 224 which is the four wheel version can use the 2CV, Dyane or Ami as the donor vehicle. A more recent variant of the 224 is the Supertourer. The Supertourer has a far larger boot and it is equipped with either a full windscreen and full weather gear or an aero-screen and tonneau cover. With flared front wings, a choice of wire wheels or Bugatti style steel wheels, the Supertourer has a definite retro look. In addition, there is a Lomax 424 which is based on the

Ami chassis but will also fit the 2CV and Dyane chassis.

Pembleton

This is another British kit car conversion available in 3 or 4 wheel versions and another car inspired by the Morgans of the 1930s. The Pembleton really does look like a vintage sports car and there are many extras that can be fitted to make it look the part such as bonnet straps, wire wheels and leather seats.

The body panels though are decidedly modern being cut from aluminium although the engine and gearbox, suspension and braking system are taken from the donor 2CV. Very occasionally, Pembletons have been built using a car other than a 2CV

In addition to these main kit cars versions, there are a number of more obscure conversions on the road. These include the Azelle which is not dissimilar to the Hoffmann, and

the Leman, also a cabriolet. Louis Barbour has brought out a British 4-wheel drive car that tested very favourably against the Land Rover on the television show 'Top Gear'. In fact it thrashed it and in a race in excellent muddy conditions in the English countryside, it resoundingly beat the heavier car. The Cygnus (swan) is a moulded polyester kit car with running boards and optional extras similar to the Pembleton. The

Alveras is another car that uses the running gear of the 2CV but the body has the styling of a vintage car, in fact this car has the definite look of a circus clown's car and the Voglietta is a Dutch designed car inspired by the 1940s.

There are many more conversions on the road as well as one-offs that people have built themselves. One particularly unusual one considering the bhp of the 2CV is a stretch limo.

There are only a handful of these cars in Britain. They consist of a standard 2CV with an added mid section that enables them to have three rows of seat. I am not sure how long it would take to go from 0-60mph, or if that is feasible anyhow!

And finally there is a club, the Citroën Specials Club devoted entirely to people who are interested in building or have built a kit car based on the Citroën 'A' series.

Information can be found at:

www.Citroënspecialsclub.org.

Clubs And Events

The 2CV club in Great Britain – 2CVGB – was founded in 1978 and presently has just under 3,000 members. It is the club for everyone interested in 2CVs and their derivatives and is run on strict lines as it is now a limited company. 2CVGB offers its members a full colour monthly club magazine with details about forthcoming events, write ups about anything 'A' series related, technical articles, trade and private adverts. In addition the club has a spare parts section that tries to source or re-manufacture essential car parts that are no longer available.

Members of 2CVGB come from far and wide and not just from Britain although the majority do. There are some 50 local groups affiliated to 2CVGB and each group will hold club meetings and events so throughout the year there is always something happening in the 2CV calendar. All

ABOVE
Convoying to
Tan Hill

events are open to everyone, whatever type of vehicle they drive. As we saw earlier, the Citroën Specials Club has its own series of events intended for drivers of kit cars based on the 2CV but again any 'A' series driver is welcome to attend. In addition there are a couple Citroën owners' clubs, but these are for owners of any Citroën car from the classics right up to modern models.

Within 2CVGB, there are also a number of 'registers'. These are sections of the club devoted to a particular type of vehicle; thus for example there is a register for the H-Van, the Dyane, the Ami, the Bijou, Van, Modcon and Méhari as well as registers for pre 1970 2CVs, drum brake 2CVs and disc brake 2CVs. Each register co-ordinator has a great deal of knowledge about their specific vehicle and keeps a list of vehicles appropriate to their register so that they can monitor the number of cars of each model in existence. They can also facilitate owners getting in touch with each other and exchanging ideas.

2CVGB officially recognise three large events which take place annually. The first main one of the season is the London to Brighton run. The very first run took place in 1984 and the idea then and still is for all the cars to be in convoy; therefore the event is held on a May Bank Holiday Sunday to avoid congesting the roads as far as is possible. It truly is a sight to behold – dozens and dozens of colourful cars all in convoy. Over the years, the start point for this magnificent run has changed; it's been as far ranging as Battersea Park, London Irish Rugby Ground in Sunbury, Esher High School and Esher College,

ABOVE
Having fun

Grasshoppers Rugby Club, Isleworth and most recently the Ace Café on the North Circular Road. The route out has also had some minor changes but the highlight of the run for some was the chug up the South Downs to Devil's Dyke with its stunning views, but not a place to miss a gear or break down! After Devil's Dyke it was a relief to take the run down into Hove Park.

Each London to Brighton run has a theme with past topics covering famous detectives, James Bond, the sixties, cowboys and Indians, school sports day and on safari. The idea behind this is that people attending will put on fancy dress and also some have been known to decorate their cars according to the relevant theme and there are prizes for the best dressed person or car. In addition to the fun side of things, a number of traders usually take a stand at the event and here much parting of money takes place with people buying items for their cherished cars costing from pence up to hundreds of pounds. Frequently, sale cars will be on display so there is always the temptation for an impulse purchase!

The next big event is Registers' Day. Usually held in June or July this event differs from the London to Brighton run as its aim is to exhibit your car. As a static show, 2CVs and other 'A' series vehicles compete in their class for the greatest number of votes from all the visitors. It's not always the most immaculate or concours condition car that wins, it's the one that the majority of people like best for whatever reason. There is one category though for the 'Masterclass' and this is for any car that has won their own category at least twice before. Also at Registers Day, there is always a large trade area so that people

can buy all those necessary items that they forgot about earlier in the year!

The final event and probably the one that achieves the highest turn out of vehicles is the 2CVGB National. This is held in a different part of the country every year and visitors from overseas regularly attend. It takes place over the August Bank Holiday and is a camping weekend. This is the place to socialise and meet up with friends and have fun. Usually there is at least one run out to a place of interest and other events or competitions take place on site. As all the arrangements are done by a team of volunteers, what takes place differs from year to year. Again there is a trade area for those final bits and pieces that the 2CV owner must have before winter sets in.

There are a number of regular meetings that 2CVGB do not officially endorse but which many 2CVers either participate in or attend. It has been traditional though for there to be a 2CV stand at the Classic Car Show held annually at the NEC, Birmingham. Here upwards of 150 car clubs put on displays with more than 1,000 vehicles and it can take more than a day to properly see

everything. The team who organise the 2CV display use their ingenuity and always aim for something interesting and perhaps a little out of the ordinary, so much so that the 2CV stand has won The Classic & Sportscar award for Best Club Event.

The Bristol Classic Car Show held at the Royal Bath & West Show Ground is another event which the 2CV fraternity participate in. The group local to the area, usually set up and man the stand at this, the longest running classic car show in the UK.

In addition to these national events, local groups organise all manner

of activities: weekend camps in the summer or winter; there are some hardy souls who find camping in the snow pleasurable, driving to the highest pubs in England, Scotland and Wales in the depths of winter, having a beach barbeque on Hayling Island on New Year's Day, scenic drives and convoys and of course pub meets.

The local groups themselves have some wonderfully imaginative names and over the years we have seen groups come and go but the names remain inventive – *Dorset Dipsticks, Pompey Puddleducks, Thames Tortoises, Souwescargots, Cambridge Legless Frogs, Leics-Car-Go* – the list can go on and on.

As well as activities in the UK, there are many overseas events that are of interest to 2CV owners and fans. Every two years, there is a World Meeting; the venue has always been in Europe from places as diverse as Scotland, Sweden, Czech Republic, Italy, Greece, Portugal and of course France. 2011 saw the 19th World Meeting take place in Salbris, France and Spain will be the host for the subsequent World Meeting in 2013. Every World Meeting attracts

thousands of visitors from all across the globe and attendees do come from as far away as Japan, Australia and America. Cars and vans in all shapes, sizes, colours and versions are on show and it is an absolute delight for any 2CV enthusiast to attend.

Though the World Meeting is the largest, there are a number of events that don't fall far behind. The French National is one of them and although in 2011 it was combined with the World Meeting, in previous years it has been an outstanding success with thousands of cars attending and thousands of visitors taking part. Again, the event takes place in a different part of France each year and inevitably wherever it happens, it becomes part of the community's social scene and local people organise special activities and participate in events, whether they have a 2CV or not.

Popular and successful events are held on a regular basis in other European countries from visiting the Arctic Circle in Sweden and Finland in winter to basking in the sunshine of Greece in the summer. There is always something going on that will please somebody.

Races And Rallies

A small, fragile looking car hardly seems to be a contender as a race car but 2CV racing is a very popular sport, supported by many, but participated in by a few. It's one motor sport that is relatively affordable to partake in; the cars don't cost a great deal initially and the basic modifications required are none too expensive. It's also a great spectator sport as the cars don't travel at excessive speeds. Despite this, drivers, marshals and spectators do take it very seriously.

In the 1960s, Citroën organised 'rally raids' which were endurance races. These were not intended solely for 2CVs but as the car was tough and able to withstand extremes of temperature, a rally over thousands of miles did not deter 2CV drivers. They were just as keen to participate in endurance rallies across continents as drivers of flashier cars.

In the 1970s, the idea of 2CV Cross came about with the first event taking place near Argenton–sur–Creuse in France. 2CV Cross is off-road racing and it was immensely popular first in France before becoming popular in most of northern Europe. The car used was a standard 2CV, Dyane, Méhari or Ami with the original engine although modifications to the gearbox could be made allowing for ten different gear ratios and for safety reasons the windscreens were removed and an anti-roll bar fitted. Drivers also had to wear crash helmets and a safety harness. 2CV Cross events probably had their heyday in the 1970s when thousands of drivers regularly competed in events all across Europe. Nowadays 2CV Cross hardly exists at all as cars are scarcer and more treasured and in its place has come circuit racing.

2CV circuit racing was popular in Europe but it wasn't until 1989 that the first race was held in Britain. At that very first event at Mallory Park, there were 22 2CVs on the grid. Since then the sport has gone from strength to strength and events take place in Britain throughout the summer in places as diverse as Anglesey Racing Circuit

(previously known as Ty Croes), Oulton Park, Silverstone and Snetterton and previously Mondello Park, the spiritual home of 2CV 24-hour racing,

Mondello Park near Dublin was the venue for the first ever 24-hour 2CV race. This took place in 1990 and this is where it stayed until 2003 before moving to Snetterton in Norfolk. The 24-hour race is really the showcase race in the 2CV racing calendar and there could be as many as forty cars on the starting grid with the drivers ranging from professionals to amateurs. It takes a special kind of person to drive through the night trying to fit in as many laps as possible. Successful teams can reach upwards of 500 laps. With just a touch of irony in its title, the club magazine of the Classic

2CV Racing Club is called 'Snail's Pace'.

Drag racing and 2CVs sounds like an oxymoron but the sport does exist. Admittedly the cars used are specials but they are adapted 2CV. What about the rural sport of 2CV tractor pulling? This takes place periodically in France and the certain modifications are made to a 2CV, it's quite a bit modification in fact, the cars are fitted with a V8 engine!

Can you imagine a 2CV in a Grand Prix race? In Argentina, the Classic Grand Prix takes place annually. Well, it's not a Grand Prix event in the traditional sense of the word; instead it's a 4000km trek through Patagonia. But rallies and treks are nothing new in the 2CV world.

In the 1950s, the 2CV broke the world altitude record when drivers

Jacques Cornet and Henri Lochon drove their car to the top of Mount Chacaltaya in the Andes, a height of 5395 metres. Admittedly they did have to get out and push the car up some of the steeper sections but it must be remembered that their car was fitted with the 375cc engine. In fact, it was an ordinary production car and the only special equipment was an additional fuel tank. This test of endurance took place while they were on an expedition that took them from Quebec in Canada, across America coast to coast finishing at Tierra del Fuego, the southernmost point of South America, a journey of some 52,000km. Cornet and Lochon drove some 1300km further south than any vehicle had travelled to before.

Another modest jolly was undertaken by French students Jean-Claude Baudot and Jacques Séguéla who were the first to drive around the world! They left Paris in October 1958 in their 425cc AZ and returned there the following November having driven more than 100,000km and having crossed eight deserts, five mountain ranges and fifty countries. It is said that they went through 36 tyres and 5,000 litres of petrol.

By the 1970s, Citroën realised that the versatility and practicality of their quirky little cars could be enhanced upon by sponsoring a rally raid. These were endurance races and were not intended solely for 2CVs but as the car was so robust, a rally over thousands of miles did not deter 2CV drivers. They were just as keen to participate in endurance rallies across continents as drivers of bigger and more powerful cars.

The first event sponsored by Citroën was the Paris to Kabul in Afghanistan and return rally. Citroën estimated that the journey would take 28 days. The route that the cars had to take was a particularly difficult one via Switzerland, Italy, Yugoslavia, Bulgaria, Turkey, Iran

and Afghanistan, a route that had been undertaken some years earlier by half track vehicles. In total 494 cars, all of them either 2CVs, Dyanes or Méharis registered for the experience. The event was aimed at the young and every participant was under thirty years of age. At the finish, 320 cars completed the course in the allotted time.

The following year, a raid to Persepolis was arranged. Five hundred 2CVs travelled from Les Halles outside Paris to Southern Iran. This again was a particularly tough event and those taking part were encouraged to take photos of their trials and tribulations and these were entered into a competition and the winning entries were given new cars.

The final and probably the most impressive 2CV rally took place in 1973. Called the Raid Afrique, it was limited to 602cc cars under five years old. Hundreds of people wanted to participate but it was limited to 60 cars and 100 people, all of them again quite young. The entrants on this epic route began their journey in the Place de la Concorde in Paris before heading to Le Havre and the sea crossing to Africa.

RIGHT
This 'Toy' sports
adventure bars

From Abidjan on the Ivory Coast, the contestants had to travel through the Tenere and Hoggar deserts of the Sahara, inhospitable featureless landscapes. The crews of the 2CVs had to be self sufficient, carrying enough water, supplies and fuel for several days. All the contestants reached their destination of Tunisia on time having covered 8,000km over tracks, dirt roads and flat sandy expanses. Every single car survived without any major damage.

In the intervening years, endurance rallies and raids have taken place in the following areas: 1991 Morocco, 1993 Raid St Amand, St Petersburg, 1994 Portugal, 1997 Sinai, 2000 Argentina, 2001 back again in Morocco, 2005 the Andes, 2007 Patagonia, 2009 Mongolia and China and last but not least Brazil in October 2011. In addition to these rallies, many individuals and small groups organise rallies or participate in rallies that are not specifically for 2CVs, rallies such as the Paris or Cassis to Dakar, Raid Australia, Raid Poronkusema (Lapland), Plymouth to Bamako, Touareg Trail, Gumball, Eight Ball Rally and Monte Carlo Rally to name just a few.

The Car's The Star

'The car's the star', well in a number of films the 2CV really was the star. As we saw earlier, a yellow 2CV took a leading role in the 1991 James Bond movie 'For Your Eyes Only' saving the hero, played by Roger Moore from a group of henchmen. But it was not just in this film that the 2CV had a starring role. In fact, in the 2002 Spanish film 'Alla rivoluzione sulla 2CV' (Off to the Revolution in a 2CV), a yellow 2CV is the star of the show. This film was subtitled into many European languages including English and the plot concerns a trio of young friends who decide to travel from France to Portugal to enjoy the first few days of liberty after the fall of António de Oliveira Salazar one of the longest lasting dictators. Although the subject of the film sounds serious, many of the road trip scenes are decidedly comedic.

Another comedy film featuring a 2CV is 'Revenge of the Pink Panther'. In this film, starring Peter Sellars as

ABOVE
On the streets of Warsaw

LEFT
Celebrating the 60th anniversary of the 2CV

Inspector Clouseau, the car is referred to as the 'Silver Hornet. This is obviously a tongue in cheek reference to the Green Hornet, a masked vigilante and his side-kick Kato. The 'Silver Hornet' or 2CV as it really is, was equipped with fancy looking features but despite this was completely useless and fell apart almost instantly whenever it was used. As we know 2CVs are tough little cars and at the end of the film, if you look carefully when the 'Silver Hornet' falls apart for the final time, you can actually see a piece of string attached to the bonnet which was used to pull it off.

A 2CV makes an appearance in Francis Ford Coppola's 'Apocalypse Now', an epic film set in Cambodia

during the Vietnam War. A 2CV from the early 1960s is crossing a bridge when it comes under air attack and to the strains of Wagner's Ride of the Valkyries is rocketed off the bridge. A 2CV is also blown up in another war film, 'The Quiet American' starring Michael Caine. Here, the car used is a pale blue model which looks as though it was built in Vietnam. This is allegedly

the very first act of terrorism during the Vietnamese civil war in 1952. A nice green and white Dolly with a green and white striped roof and registration number D672 XMO takes a starring role in the 2004 film 'Dead Man's Shoes'.

One film that has very many scenes featuring the 2CV is the French film 'Les Amants' (The Lovers) starring

Jeanne Moreau. This film from 1958 was quite controversial at the time, but that besides, it's a brilliant show case for the 2CV as a fair bit of the action and dialogue takes place in the car. The final scene shows the two protagonists driving down a country lane in a 2CV.

Not many of the cars used in films are as original. Quite often, apart from extras put on specifically for the film, the car may not be the correct model for the year that the film is set in or have strange additions that the cognoscenti would be aware of. Such is the case in 'Indecent Proposal' which features a 4 light 2CV with a style of hood that wasn't used until the 1970s and also in American Graffiti. In the latter film, a 2CV with a French nationality sticker (F) is seen in America at a time of big Buicks and Chevrolets and at a time when the car wasn't even sold in America. The film is set in 1962 but the car used is much newer than that, probably a 1967 model.

It's not just on the big screen that the 2CV has found fame. The 2CV has featured in countless television shows ranging from 'Ashes to Ashes' where a green 2CV with a red roof is a background feature in just one episode to 'The Professionals' which used a variety of 2CVs and Dyanes in many episodes. In addition the animated shows 'South Park' and 'Charlie Brown' have also featured 2CVs. Tintin, a Belgian reporter featuring in a series of comic strips drawn by Hergé uses a 2CV among many cars on his travels.

And of course there is the television show 'Top Gear'. Jeremy Clarkson allegedly intensely dislikes the car and once referred to them as a "weedy, useless little engine" yet maybe he is a secret 2CV admirer as 2CVs feature reasonably frequently on the show. The one episode featuring a 2CV that springs to mind was when the Top Gear team, but mainly Richard Hammond tried to see what would happen to two cars, a Ford Mondeo and a 2CV Bamboo if they got caught in the full power from the engines of a Boeing 747. With 58,000 pounds of thrust, the inevitable was bound to happen and both cars were blown off course and completely destroyed. Regrettably, this little jape ruined what seemed to be a perfectly good car and it is one episode that will be forever etched in our hearts.

Museums
And Collections

As we saw earlier, Lane Motor Museum in Nashville, Tennessee has the one and only Cogolin on display. But they also have a right hand drive 2CV Yacco replica, a vehicle that was never put into production. Yacco Oil was the original oil distributor for Citroën in the forties and fifties and Citroën teamed up with them to run an endurance test using a 2CV. In addition, Lane Motor Museum has in their collection a red van that was used by the Belgian postal service. The van is also right hand drive, something that the Belgian postmen liked as it enabled them to pop out of the driver's seat and straight onto the pavement. In addition a number of 2CVs including a ripple bonnet and Sahara, Dyane, H Van, Bijou, Ami 6 and Ami 8 as well as a couple of Méharis are on display.

Nearer to home there are a couple of fantastic collections in France. There is one in Alsace which was created by the local 2CV group in 1998. Unfortunately it is only open on Saturdays but it is well worth a visit with its huge collection of cars spanning the history of the 2CV. All cars on display are in the exact condition they were in when the museum acquired them. Unusually for a museum, there is an attached spare parts shop where spare parts can be purchased and where cars in the process of being dismantled are kept.

The Citromuseum, north of Cannes in Provence has a collection of some fifty cars, all low mileage and in original or as close to original, unrestored condition. The aim of Henri Fradet who started the collection is to keep a record of all that Citroën had manufactured and to have a collection of rare and unusual cars before they were lost

forever. 2CVs, Dyanes, Méharis and Acadianes feature in the collection along with other Citroën models.

In 1928, on the avenue des Champs-Elysées, Citroën opened a glass-façaded showroom dedicated to displaying either its most recent or most interesting vehicles. This building called Hippo-Citroën is quite an oddity as it is a combination of a car showroom and museum. For the 60th birthday celebrations for the 2CV, it had a nostalgia tinted homage to the 2CVs as did the Cité des Sciences et de l'Industrie. Hopefully when the 2CVs 70th birthday comes round, there will be as much interest in these peculiar cars for these sorts of displays to continue.

The pièce de résistance where 2CV collections are concerned is Le Conservatoire in Paris. It is entirely based on Citroën cars and 2CVs jostle for space with anything from prototypes and concept cars to the Traction Avant, the DS to the Nemo, in fact any vehicle from 1919 to the present day. The very last right hand drive built Dolly is on display. Le Conservatoire is not really a museum as it does not open to the public but it does loan vehicles

for display purposes. In addition to the vehicles, Le Conservatoire also has an archive where there is a vast collection taking up almost 1½ kilometres of shelf space. Here can be found all manner of advertising materials, drawings, designs, registers of vehicle chassis numbers, old picture, films and books devoted to André Citroën and the brand he founded.

Buying A 2CV

If this book has whetted your appetite and made you think how great it would be to own one of these traditional yet idiosyncratic cars, the following is a guide to some of the things that need to be taken into consideration. Now that they have been out of production for over twenty years, there are fewer and fewer cars available and the price is rising exponentially. The days when a 2CV could be snapped up for a couple of hundred pounds are long gone but bargains are still out there. However if you are interested in a fully renovated and perfectly restored model, the price could reach as high as £10,000!

RIGHT
In need of some
tender loving care

But back to the pitfalls and also advantages of owning a 2CV. The first thing any prospective owner must realise that these cars are driven, there is no ABS, power steering, catalytic converter etc, however there could be plenty of noise and unexpected ventilation. The car was designed to work for its living so there are few refinements and the car is practical, down to earth with no frills. As we saw earlier the later cars built in Portugal tend to be of inferior quality and though the French built cars may be older, they will have overcome the depredations of time much better.

The very first thing to look at is the chassis. Unlike many other cars, the body of the 2CV is built completely on the chassis, a ladder-shaped construction that generally includes a plate on top and one on the bottom. These coverings make it impossible to see what the internal state of the chassis is like and an ordinary steel chassis may rust after just a few years. A galvanised chassis is usually guaranteed for ten years and so it is preferable to buy a car with a galvanised chassis. The main danger points to be aware of are the two legs of the chassis which carry the engine.

If rust has got into the joints, this will weaken and bend them in time. If the chassis is shot to pieces, the car can be rejected although replacement chassis are easily available and replacements can be fitted either by the experts or as a DIY project. But it must be a good after market chassis designed to Citroën specifications from a reliable source as there are some inferior ones around that are made of poor quality metal and so are weak. There are others that do not fit properly and where the holes that are drilled are out of alignment and of course general poor workmanship is another consideration. If a chassis has been pre-welded or previously plated more than twice before, it should be rejected as this implies that there could be a lot more rust inside the chassis than is visible on the outside. Changing a chassis is a task that doesn't require a lot of mechanical knowledge although it can be a time consuming job if as may happen you are faced with seized bolts and the like.

After the initial cursory glance at the body, it is a good idea to have a thorough and detailed look for signs of rust. The strip under the front windscreen is prone to rust which can ultimately lead to ingress of water into the car. Although it isn't a terribly difficult job to replace this ventilator flap, it is rather fiddly. The door sills which support the outer edge of the car and the inner floors are another area to look at and they should be rust free or as near to rust free as possible. Note should be particularly aimed at the 'A', 'B' and 'C' pillars (the pillars that separate the doors) where they meet the sills. The front seat belt mountings are bolted to the sills and it is important that the inner sills are sound. The rear seat belts which are generally lap belts are mounted on a bolt set into the front of the inner rear wing. This area needs to be checked and it should be rust free..

Rust has a tendency to rot the floor pans. This is usually due to water and dirt getting embedded into any carpet that has been laid. If the original rubber mats are in position, they cover the entire floor and will sweat and cause condensation which in turn causes damp and ultimately rust. Cars are often repaired in these sections, and if the workmanship is good, cars should not be turned down if they have replacement

floor pans. The floor also needs to be sound for the seat runners to be able to be bolted firmly to the floor so that they can run smoothly.

The spare wheel is located in the boot, apart from the Sahara, and the floor here also needs to be checked for rust because road water can splash up and corrode the bottom edge of the boot and the spare wheel well. Many 2CV owners have added a wooden or plywood boot floor as this hides away

the spare wheel and gives a good level surface.

All body parts are bolted on and are therefore easily replaceable so if the car that you yearn for has rusty doors or a rusty bonnet, boot or wings, these can be repaired or replaced sometimes even with brand new. Wings made out of GRP that does not rust have been available. With regard to changing external parts, even plastic headlamp shells are available should the original metal ones become damaged or go rusty.

Any tears, splits, fraying or leaks in the roof are not a major issue as currently roofs are available from a number of suppliers who provide them in different materials and a multitude of colours. It is also possible to arrange for a heated rear window to be fitted into the roof nowadays. Changing a roof is not an onerous job at all.

The engine and gearbox of a 2CV should be clean and dry and free of oil

RIGHT
Resting on the
Scilly Isles

leaks. There should be four cardboard heater tubes; two large ones that take the heat from the heat exchangers into the car and two smaller black ones, one on each side that take the excess air out under the wings. These tubes should be fitted properly and should be in good condition.

A 2CV engine has a very distinctive, sweet sound, a putt…putt… but beware of any untoward noises as this could mean trouble. The gearbox should operate smoothly without any crunching sounds but it must be noted that there is no synchromesh in first gear. The engines are tough and tend to work better when in use frequently so a high mileage engine is not something necessarily to avoid. 2CV engines do not like to be left idle for long periods.

Heavy or stiff steering could be something simple like low front tyre pressure or it could be more serious like a bent chassis and so we are back to the beginning. If none of this has put you off and you go ahead and buy a car, it should give you years and years of fun and cheap motoring. And while you are out on the road don't forget to wave at other 2CV owners.

Rebirth

Many of today's major car manufacturers have tried to harness the charm and style of their old cars with updated versions incorporating retro looks. We have the new Beetle, the Fiat 500 and the MINI to name just a few. Citroën have tried this as well and their first foray into designing a vehicle reminiscent of the 2CV was the C3 Pluriel. This car with its modular body and bizarre electric fully retractable roof was nothing like the car it tried to imitate. For a start to fully convert it into a convertible, the huge roof bars had to be removed but there was nowhere to store them in the car, so they had to be left behind but the roof couldn't be put up without them. Innovative, but unlike the 2CV not at all practical.

The C-Cactus was a prototype car that Citroën showed to the world at the 2007 Frankfurt Motor Show. Although it was a diesel hybrid, it did have overtones of the 2CV. It was produced with many recycled parts

and was intended to have great fuel economy, but unfortunately the project never fully came off the ground and eventually sank without trace.

In 2009, the concept REVOLTe hybrid was shown at the Frankfurt Motor Show. Again, this was a car inspired by the 2CV but it was nothing like the original being bright and almost gaudy and full of all manner of gadgets and luxurious items, a sort of modern trendy 2CV if such a thing could exist. Though the REVOLTe didn't go into production, what was conceived was the new DS series of cars based on the REVOLTe but with overtones of the original DS from the 1950s onwards. Despite grooves in its bonnet similar to the original 2CV, this car too is nothing like the original. So as yet there has been no modern reincarnation of the 2CV. We will just have to wait and see what Citroën has in its planning pipeline and if they do join the growing band of retro stylers.

Things You Didn't Know

1. The eccentric sport of welly wanging has been given a scientific makeover. A team of boffins have built a machine to enable the welly to be thrust to nearly 80 metres by using the gearbox from a 2CV combined with the engine from a concrete mixer.

2. Beware of singer songwriter Billy Joel if you should ever meet him on the open road. He has had a spate of crashes including once damaging his 1967 black and burgundy Charleston when he lost control in wet conditions. And he was only going out to buy a pizza.

3. Citroën made their first tests of hydropneumatic suspension on a 2CV in 1944.

4. One of the most bizarre specials ever made was a 2CV van crossed with a

Ferrari. Called the Citrrari, this was a weird 189mph hybrid! Why anyone would want to create such a vehicle is beyond imagination, but it was used as a promotional vehicle for the Nimik racing team. The Ferrari chosen was the F355 with its 3.5 litre V8 engine and an adapted 2CV body was positioned on top. The resulting vehicle was able to go from 0-60mph in less than five seconds. The whole operation took around 1,500 hours to complete and cost in the region of £156,000.

5. The 2CV was the first car that Citroën advertised on television – the year, 1968.

6. Lloyd Cole, the English singer songwriter penned a song all about the 2CV called appropriately enough '2CV' and the song starts with the words 'She drove her mother's car, 'twas a 2CV.

7. The Dyane was named after the Greek goddess.

8. The chevron logo in Citroën advertising was blue and yellow until the 1980s when it was changed to white on a red background.

9. In France, during the 1950s, a new 2CV was delivered with a free third party, fire and theft five day insurance.

10. A motorbike and sidecar combination has been made out of a 2CV. Called the Millennium Bug, the bike can be ridden or driven. It consists of a Citroën GSA 1300 engine and a Cossack Ural gearbox. The side car is a narrowed and shortened 2CV with a steering wheel and all the foot pedals inside which are linked to the motorbike.

11. On British built 2CVs, the speedo

was placed in the centre of the console unlike the French cars where it was strapped to the door pillar!

12. The American actor Woody Harrelson has owned 2CVs.

13. The characteristic corrugated body of early 2CVs was inspired by German Junkers aircraft.

14. André Citroën set up the first European consumer credit company, Socav.

15. Quentin Wilson, the television presenter and motoring enthusiast allegedly once said that 2CVs should be available on prescription from the NHS for depression! Quentin Wilson is also an honorary member of 2CVGB.

ACKNOWLEDGEMENTS

In my quest for information for this book, I have received help and advice from a number of people, but in particular I would like to thank my husband Dave for his extensive knowledge of the subject, Richard Maconnachie for his wonderful photos and all the members of the SAS (Swindon Association of Snails) for their support and encouragement.

Ellie Charleston, author

To download our latest catalogue and to view
the full range of books and DVDs visit:

www.G2ent.co.uk

The pictures in this book were provided courtesy of the following:

RICHARD MACONNACHIE

SHUTTERSTOCK
www.shutterstock.com

Design and artwork by David Wildish and Scott Giarnese

Published by G2 Entertainment Limited

Publishers Jules Gammond and Edward Adams

Written by Ellie Charleston